The Sphinx

Other titles in the Monsters and Mythical Creatures series include:

Monsters
and Mythical Creatures

The Sphinx

Stuart A. Kallen

ReferencePoint
Press®

San Diego, CA

© 2012 ReferencePoint Press, Inc.
Printed in the United States

For more information, contact:
ReferencePoint Press, Inc.
PO Box 27779
San Diego, CA 92198
www.ReferencePointPress.com

LIBRARY OF CONGRESS CATALOGING-IN-PUBLICATION DATA

Kallen, Stuart A., 1955-
  The sphinx : part of the Monsters and mythical creatures series / by Stuart A. Kallen.
    p. cm. — (Monsters and mythical creatures series)
  Includes bibliographical references and index.
  ISBN-13: 978-1-60152-222-1 (hardback)
  ISBN-10: 1-60152-222-3 (hardback)
  1. Sphinxes (Mythology) I. Title. II. Series: Monsters and mythical creatures.
  BL820.S66K35 2012
  398.45—dc23
                                                                    2011026636

4967 6132 9/12

Contents

Half Human, Half Beast

Five thousand years ago wild lions were among the most numerous mammals on the planet. Lions were found in Europe, the Americas, and in great numbers in Africa. As one of the earth's most dangerous land animals, lions were feared and hunted—and revered as deities. In ancient Egypt, more than 4,500 years ago, lions were worshipped for their ferocious strength and protective abilities. During this era, ancient Egyptians carved lion paws into chair legs and built beds in the shape of the animal's outstretched body to ward off bad luck and harmful spirits.

Did You Know?

Egyptologists believe the Great Sphinx is the largest stone sculpture ever made by humans.

When a pharaoh marched off to battle, a tamed lion was often by his side. This creature was not viewed as a pet but a living representation of the goddess Sekhmet, who had the body of a woman and the head of a lioness. Sekhmet was worshipped as a fierce hunter with no equal. It was believed that her breath created the Sahara Desert and that she protected pharaohs during times of war. Little wonder then that sometime around 2550 BC, the ancient Egyptians carved a huge statue that fused a lion and a human, creating a single powerful creature called the Great Sphinx. At 66 feet (20 m) in height, the statue is taller than a modern six-story building. It was constructed to guard and protect the great pyramids located in Giza next to the Nile River. At least that is what modern historians commonly believe.

Although the Egyptians kept detailed records about nearly every aspect of life, no writings were ever found explaining the symbolism of the Great Sphinx of Giza. Historians have discovered ancient religious texts, government records, lesson plans, historical tales, and even recipes and love letters. But evidence of who ordered the construction of the sphinx and why has never been found.

For much of its existence, the Great Sphinx was only a head sticking out of the sand. The colossus, or huge statue, was partially excavated around 1400 BC, but within a century the body had again disappeared under blowing sands. It remained buried until the twentieth century when a French Egyptologist cleared away tons of sand to reveal the colossus as it had appeared to the ancient Egyptians.

The facial features of the Great Sphinx have been described in various ways over the centuries by poets, philosophers, and tourists.

Egypt's majestic Great Sphinx, a structure that is part human and part lion, rises from the desert sands of Giza. The purpose of the Great Sphinx has been lost to time as has the name of its creator.

Between the sixteenth and nineteenth centuries, European travelers repeatedly wrote that the colossus had the face of a woman, while modern historians believe the features are male. Some say the sphinx has the face of Isis, the Egyptian goddess of nature and magic, others think it is the pharaoh Khafre, who ordered construction of the Great Pyramid of Giza around 2550 BC. Whatever or whoever inspired the creation of the Great Sphinx, the colossus is one of the most recognizable images in the world.

Monsters and Guardians

The meaning and origins of the word *sphinx* are nearly as mysterious as the statue itself. No one knows what the sphinx was called when it was created, but historians speculate that the ancient Egyptians used the word *seshepankh* to describe the statue. This term translates as "living image"—the ancients believed the statue to be the living image of the pharaoh Khafre or possibly the living image of Atum, the ancient god of creation. Archeologists conjecture that when the Greeks began visiting Egypt around 550 BC they corrupted the word *seshepankh* to *sphingo*, or "sphinx" in English. In Greek, *sphingo* means to squeeze, tighten up, or strangle. The word might have been coined by those who observed sphinxlike lions biting and strangling their prey.

> ## Did You Know?
> Wind, humidity, and smog are causing the Great Sphinx to crumble and shrink in size.

The classical Greeks recast the role of the sphinx, much as they likely changed the word to describe it. In Greek mythology sphinxes are stranglers, man-eating monsters with the wings of an eagle or the tail of a snake. And for the past five centuries, sphinxes have appeared in Western art and literature as symbols of magic, danger, luck, secrecy, and beauty.

Whatever the meanings and mysteries behind sphinxes, the idea of a creature half human and half animal has stirred feelings of fear, wonder, destiny, and distress for countless centuries. The creature has captured humanity's collective imagination, and visitors to the Great Sphinx often ponder if the answers to life's riddles are behind the creature's knowing smile.

Chapter 1

The Egyptian Sphinx

One day a young prince was hunting in Egypt's Valley of Gazelles southeast of Giza. While walking at noon in the hot desert sun the prince could see the Great Sphinx standing guard in front of the Pyramid of Khafre, the second largest of the three monumental pyramids on the Giza plateau. The weary prince, who was the son of the pharaoh Amenhotep II, decided to rest in the shadow of the Great Sphinx. At the time, the sphinx was buried up to its neck by drifting desert sands. Only the head protruded above the surface. The statue was crowned with a headdress called a *nemes*, a royal kerchief folded in a manner exclusive to pharaohs. The *nemes* on the sphinx spread out on both sides like a lion's mane.

While resting in the shade, the prince dozed off and had a dream in which a great stone sphinx came alive. The prince recognized the creature as the embodiment of the god Horemakhet (also written as Horem-Akhet). The dream deity told the prince: "The sand of the desert whereon I am laid has covered me. Save me."[1] Horemakhet made a promise to the prince: If he cleared away the sand and repaired the body of the Great Sphinx he would become the ruler of Egypt.

After the prince awoke, he ordered the excavation of the sphinx's body. For months, workmen struggled to clear away sand in front of the huge stone statue while adding new limestone blocks to repair the paws and chest. Shortly thereafter, in 1401 BC, the prince's dream came true and he was crowned pharaoh Thutmosis IV. In commemoration of the event, Thutmosis erected an imposing 15-ton stone slab (13.6 metric tons) between the front paws of the sphinx as the centerpiece for a chapel.

The stone slab, called a Dream Stela, contains picture writing symbols, or hieroglyphs, that tell the story of the pharaoh's dream. The stela, which is 12 feet (3.6 m) high, 7 feet (2.1 m) wide, and 2 feet (.6 m) thick, faces east toward the rising sun. An intricate sculpture cut into the stone surface, called a bas-relief, decorates the top of the stela. The artwork contains images from Thutmosis's dream in which two sphinxes are seated on pedestals back-to-back in a mirror image of one another. Two pharaohs hold out offerings while a large set of wings stretch out above the entire design.

The 15-ton stone tablet, or Dream Stela, that sits between the paws of the Great Sphinx tells of a dream that foretold of Thutmosis IV's crowning as pharaoh. In his dream, the young prince learned that he would become pharaoh if he cleared the sand and repaired the body of the colossal statue.

Horus in the Horizon

The Great Sphinx of Giza was already 1,000 years old when Thutmosis had his dream. Until the stela was made, no one had ever written down the name Horemakhet to identify the statue despite the fact that hieroglyphic inscriptions had been used on hundreds of Egyptian tombs since 3200 BC. According to Egyptologist James Allen, "The Egyptians didn't write history so we have no solid evidence for what its builders thought the Sphinx was. . . . Certainly something divine, presumably the image of a king, but beyond that is anyone's guess."[2]

To Thutmosis IV, the sphinx was a magical embodiment of Horemakhet, which means Horus in the Horizon. Horus was one of the supreme deities in a pantheon that contained around 700 different gods and goddesses. Horus was often drawn as a creature with the body of a man and the head of a falcon wearing a *nemes*. In some cases Horus was portrayed with the body of a lion. The name Horus translates as "lord of the sky" or "distant one."

The ancient Egyptians believed that every aspect of their society was controlled by gods like Horus. The Nile was not viewed as a body of water but as an incarnation of the fertility god Hepi. The sun was not thought to be a burning orb in outer space but Re, the father of all beings, who raced his fiery chariot across the sky every day.

Horus was the god of the kingship and also Re's representative on Earth. When Thutmosis referred to him as Horus in the Horizon, the god was a combination of Horus and Re that represented the sunrise on the eastern horizon. Then and now, when the sun rises it casts a red glow on the face of the sphinx, bringing the god to life at the dawning of every day. The fact that this powerful god appeared to Thutmosis in a dream was of utmost importance, as Egyptologist Kasia Szpakowska explains:

> It was very unusual for a god to speak to a mortal. The kings, however, throughout Egyptian history would be spoken to by gods. They received communications from gods through

Did You Know?

Desert sands continually blow over the Great Sphinx; without frequent cleaning by modern workers, the colossus would probably be buried again within 20 to 30 years.

revelations and oracles. But seeing a god in a dream was an extremely rare phenomenon. So that's also part of the reason that Thutmosis IV erected the stela—to emphasize that he was the person whom the god chose to speak to in this very, very intimate encounter during a dream.[3]

A Royal National Park

After Thutmosis IV uncovered the Great Sphinx and carved the Dream Stela, he established a religious cult of sphinx worshippers that lasted for centuries. In cities and villages throughout the Egyptian kingdom, sphinxes were carved into stone, painted on walls, and sketched onto papyrus scrolls. Egyptologists believe the center of sphinx worship took place at a temple constructed on a small rise northeast of the Great Sphinx. The huge complex, made from mud bricks, is described by archaeologist Mark Lehner as "a kind of royal national park . . . dedicated to the Sphinx as Horemakhet."[4]

The floors of the temple were made of fine white alabaster stone. The walls were covered inside and out with beautiful granite. The sphinx temple complex included sanctuaries, called rest-houses, where pharaohs could conduct religious rituals under the gaze of the Great Sphinx. Broad terraces, called viewing platforms, allowed pharaohs, queens, princes, and other royalty to stroll in front of the colossus and view the rising sun lighting the face of the sphinx.

Other features of the temple complex include scores of small stelae that recorded the comings and goings of various nobles, religious leaders, and average citizens. Some of these commemorative stelae show a large statue of a pharaoh resting behind the Dream Stela between the sphinx's paws. While the statue is gone, archeologists estimate it must have been quite amazing, standing over 20 feet (6.1 m) tall. Some stelae refer to the Great Sphinx as *Setepet*, which translates as "the Chosen." According to Lehner, this refers to the pharaohs who were chosen to lead Egypt as symbols of the immortal Horus:

In their first year of rule, pharaohs came to the chapel between the forepaws to make dedications to the Sphinx and to be ordained and confirmed in their position. In so doing, they participated in a [merging] of royal power from living pharaoh to . . . ancient kings like Khufu and Khafre and ultimately to Horemakhet, the primeval god-king whose image towered above them in the form of the Sphinx.[5]

The sphinx temple complex was constructed near an older temple complex likely built around 1,000 years earlier, during Khafre's reign. The old temple sits directly next to the new temple. The old

Guarding the Pyramids

The Great Sphinx stands guard in front of Khafre's pyramid, one of three monumental pyramids on the Giza Plateau. The Great Pyramid of Khufu (or Cheops) is the largest. It was constructed approximately between 2560 and 2540 BC from millions of limestone blocks—each one weighing nearly 3 tons (2.7 metric tons). Many of these stones were cut from the U-shaped quarry behind the sphinx. Khufu's pyramid rises 481 feet (146 m) above the desert floor, and each side of its square base is 756 feet (230 m) in length. Until 1887, when the Eiffel Tower was constructed in Paris, the Great Pyramid was the tallest structure on Earth—a record it held for around 440 centuries.

The pyramid of Khufu's son Khafre is slightly smaller—about 471 feet (143 m) high and 705 feet (215 m) square. This pyramid was built between 2558 and 2532 BC. Most Egyptologists believe the Great Sphinx was carved in front of Khafre's pyramid around this time. Khufu's grandson Menkaure constructed the smallest of the three Giza pyramids, which is about 215 feet (65 m) high and 344 feet (105 m) square. Menkaure ruled between 2490 and 2472 BC, and the pyramid was built sometime during that period.

temple contains 24 red granite pillars, each one possibly representing an hour of the day. The old temple has two small sanctuaries, one on the east side and one on the west. Although they are only the size of closets, the west sanctuary lights up when the sun rises on the solstice (June 21–22), and the east one is illuminated when the sun sets on that day. Pillars representing the sky goddess Nut stand before the sanctuaries where she gives birth to the sun in the morning and swallows it at night.

Restoration Work

The old temple was probably buried and unknown during the time of Thutmosis IV. His workmen cleared away the sand from the front paws and built mud brick walls around the sphinx to protect it from sand and wind. Many of the original stones around the base had fallen off, and these were repaired and replaced.

Over the centuries the sand returned, and by the third century AD the Dream Stela and new temple were buried along with most of the sphinx. The stela was uncovered in 1816 by an Italian sea captain named Giambattista Caviglia, who led a team of 100 men on a four-month dig that partially uncovered the sphinx.

During the excavation of the monolith, Caviglia discovered a stone beard that had cracked off the statue. Living pharaohs often wore false beards as symbols of their power. The beard near the sphinx, however, was braided in a fashion seen only on gods and dead pharaohs. Egyptologists believe the beard was not part of the original statue but was added after its restoration during the reign of Thutmosis IV. Today the beard fragment rests in the basement of the British Museum in London where it has never been on display. Caviglia found another addition, a statue of an upright king cobra emblem called a uraeus. Archaeologists say it was once attached to the sphinx's *nemes* headdress.

The sphinx was not completely excavated for more than another century, when French Egyptologist Émile Baraize began clearing

> ## Did You Know?
>
> The meaning of Egyptian hieroglyphs was lost until 1822 when French linguist Jean-François Champollion learned to translate the picture symbols into French.

sand from the site in 1925. After 11 years of toil with primitive equipment, Baraize completely uncovered the Great Sphinx, revealing features that had not been seen in more than a millennium. At the time, Egyptian archaeologist Selim Hassan wrote in the *New York Times*, "The Sphinx has thus emerged into the landscape out of shadows of what seemed to be an impenetrable oblivion."[6]

Gaudy Colors

Most modern historians agree the Great Sphinx has the body of a lion and the head of man. The creature is couchant, or lying down with its head erect. The head is 30 feet (10 m) long and 14 feet (4 m) wide. The paws of the sphinx are 50 feet (15 m) long, with a total body length of 241 feet (73.5 m). The statue is 20 feet (6 m) wide and over 66 feet (20.2 m) high, making it the largest monolith, or stand-alone statue, in the world. It was carved from a limestone projection in a horseshoe-shaped quarry where stones were hewn for

The nose of the Great Sphinx has been missing for centuries. One well-known theory, that soldiers in Napoleon's forces blew the nose off with a cannon, has been disproven. Writings from the 1400s blame the damage on an outraged religious fanatic, but no other proof exists.

construction of the pyramids at Giza, sometime around 2550 BC. The features on the face of the sphinx are often said to be those of pharaoh Khafre, who ruled Egypt during the era when the second great pyramid was being constructed.

The nose of the sphinx, which was about 3 feet (1 m) wide, has been missing for centuries. It was long believed that after the French emperor Napoleon conquered Egypt in 1798, his soldiers blew off its nose with a cannon during a battle. However, drawings made in 1755 show the sphinx already missing its nose. In 1991 Lehner discovered writings by a fifteenth-century Arab historian, Al-Maqrizi, who said the nose was destroyed by a religious fanatic named Muhammad Sa'im al-Dahr in 1378. When Sa'im al-Dahr discovered peasants making magical offerings to the sphinx in hope of increasing their grain harvest, he was so outraged he pried the nose off.

The nose was never found, but Lehner discovered red paint residue in crevices of the face, leading to the conclusion that the sphinx was once painted entirely red. Blue and yellow paint have also been found. Evan Hadingham, senior science editor for the TV series *Nova*, concludes that "the Sphinx was once decked out in gaudy comic book colors."[7]

> **Did You Know?**
>
> At one time the head of the Great Sphinx had a hole in it about 5 feet square and 6 feet deep (1.5 m by 1.5 m by 1.8 m) probably used by ancient Egyptians to affix a headdress to the statue. The hole was filled with cement in 1925 to stabilize the head.

A Different Pharaoh's Face?

The Great Sphinx of Giza is by far the largest statue of its type but not the first one created by the ancient Egyptians. The oldest known sphinx predates the Great Sphinx by several decades. The freestanding limestone statue, about 10 feet (3 m) long, has the face of Queen Hetepheres II, who was married to Djedefre, Egypt's pharaoh from 2566 to 2558 BC.

The sphinx of Hetepheres II was discovered in the early twentieth century at the site of a now ruined pyramid constructed north of

Giza by the pharaoh Djedefre. Djedefre was the son and successor of Khufu, who ordered construction of the Great Pyramid, the largest of the three at Giza. Egyptologists have long assumed Djedefre's brother Khafre, whose pyramid sits next to the Great Pyramid, created the Great Sphinx. However, after 20 years of research Vassil Dobrev of the French Archaeological Institute in Cairo concluded the Great Sphinx might have been constructed by Djedefre. In 2004 Dobrev was the first person to speculate that the sphinx was built by Djedefre after the death of his father, Khufu: "When Khufu died, the people of ancient Egypt were weary, having spent decades building pyramids. . . . Djedefre, who succeeded Khufu as pharaoh, built the

Carving the Sphinx

When workers carved the Great Sphinx of Giza more than 45 centuries ago they did not have sturdy tools made from iron or bronze to aid them in their work. An ancient Egyptian sculptor likely used a hammer made from a fist-sized stone that was lashed to a stick with a leather strap. This was used to pound a chisel made from copper, a soft metal that dulled after only a few blows against the hard stone. In 2009, Evan Hadingham, senior science editor of the PBS TV series *Nova*, and Rick Brown, a professor of sculpture at the Massachusetts College of Art and Design, attempted to carve a scaled-down version of the sphinx using replicas of ancient tools. Hadingham noted that the copper chisels became blunt after only a few blows and required constant resharpening. Under these conditions, one laborer could probably carve about 1 square foot (.093 sq. m) of stone per week, says Brown. "At that rate," Brown says, "it would have taken 100 people three years to complete the Sphinx."

Evan Hadingham, "Riddle of the Sphinx," *Cosmos*, April 2010. www.cosmosmagazine.com.

monument in the image of his father, identifying him with the sun god Ra, as a piece of propaganda to restore respect for the dynasty."[8]

Part of Dobrev's evidence is the orientation of the Great Pyramid and the Great Sphinx. Modern tourists approach Giza from Cairo in the east and see the sphinx separate from the pyramids. In ancient times, the center of Egyptian government and culture was Memphis to the south. Visitors approaching from that direction see the sphinx in a dramatic profile with Khufu's pyramid behind it.

The Colossal Sphinx

Dobrov's theory has not been universally accepted. Most Egyptologists and archeologists maintain that Khafre built the sphinx, but the lack of written records from the era will keep experts guessing for years to come. Much more is known about sphinxes created for another ruler, Queen Hatshepsut. The massive mortuary complex she had built beneath the cliffs at Deir el Bahari contain extensive hieroglyphic records about the queen and her many successful endeavors.

Hatshepsut was one of the few female pharaohs in Egypt's male-dominated political hierarchy. During her successful 21-year reign, which began around 1479 BC, Hatshepsut oversaw a major building boom. This included her beautiful mortuary complex, constructed so her followers could continue to worship her after her death. The complex was excavated in the 1920s and 1930s, and the buildings combine extraordinary sculptures and monumental architecture. Shrines on site are dedicated to the sun god Re and also the sky goddess Hathor, represented as either a woman or a cow.

Hatshepsut's mortuary complex was originally guarded by six giant sphinxes. One of these, called the Colossal Sphinx of Hatshepsut, is now on display at the Metropolitan Museum of Art, or the Met, in

> ## Did You Know?
>
> The granite and alabaster used to build the temple of the Great Sphinx were ferried up the Nile from Aswan to Giza, a distance of 406 miles (653 km), on large barges pulled by men. No one knows how these stones were lifted onto barges without the use of hoists or cranes.

New York City. The Colossal Sphinx is a lion with Hatshepsut's face, a *nemes* headdress, and the ceremonial beard worn by all pharaohs male or female. The statue has the tail of a bull which represents the fertility of ancient Egyptian royalty. According to the Met's description of the sphinx, "The sculptor has carefully observed the powerful muscles of the lion as contrasted to the handsome and attractive idealized face of the queen."[9]

The word "colossal" accurately describes the reddish granite statue which still has traces of blue and yellow paint. The sphinx is over 11 feet (3.3 m) long, 5 feet (1.5 m) high, and weighs more than 7 tons (6.35 metric tons). Twenty years after her death, Hatshepsut's Colossal Sphinx was smashed to pieces by her stepson, the pharaoh Thutmosis III, who had been prevented from taking the throne for decades while his stepmother ruled Egypt. The sphinx, along with several others from the mortuary complex, was reconstructed by workers at the Met in the mid-twentieth century.

Queen Hatshepsut receives offerings from her people. The queen's mortuary complex, which she built so that her followers could continue their worship of her after death, was once guarded by six giant sphinxes.

A Sphinx in Reverse

In addition to her mortuary temple, Hatshepsut oversaw major construction at the Karnak temple complex in ancient Thebes. The huge site, filled with sacred buildings now in ruins, is near present-day Luxor, about 300 miles (483 km) south of Cairo. The Karnak complex contains four areas built and expanded by various pharaohs over the centuries: the Precincts of Mut, Montu, Amun-Re, and the dismantled Temple of Amenhotep IV. Today only Amun-Re is open to visitors. British Egyptologist Leonard Cottrell describes the incredible size and complexity of Karnak's four sacred precincts: "[Karnak is] a building complex that would cover much of mid-Manhattan. Within the walls of the [complex] there would be room for St. Peter's [Basilica] in Rome, the Milan Cathedral, and Notre Dame in Paris. The outer walls of [Karnak] would comfortably enclose ten European cathedrals."[10]

At Karnak Queen Hatshepsut is known for expanding the 20-acre (8 ha) Precinct of Mut. The queen believed she was the direct descendant of the mother goddess Mut, and she was a regular visitor to the temples, statues, and lake on the site. Like other Egyptian deities, Mut played different roles in Egyptian religious belief and was depicted in several guises. In her human form Mut was the protective mother goddess. In the form of the goddess Sekhmet, she was a sphinx in reverse, a lion-headed deity with the body of a human.

Sekhmet means "The Mighty One," and the deity was considered to be as powerful as Horus. Like a lion, she protected the pharaoh in battle. Sekhmet was merciless when punishing humans who angered her, and she might slaughter enemies with fiery arrows launched from heaven or visit plagues upon entire populations. Because of Sekhmet's fierce nature many rituals at the precinct of Mut were performed to appease the goddess and dissuade her from harming humans.

The High Priest of Amun

Statues and paintings of Sekhmet are among hundreds of sphinxes in the Precinct of Mut and elsewhere at Karnak. The Karnak sphinxes were placed there during different periods of ancient Egyptian history, often centuries apart. One of the most dramatic sphinx displays was installed around 1070 BC when Egypt was wracked by chaos and war. At the time, the country was divided into two nations, north and south. The southern part of Egypt was ruled by Pinedjem, a high priest of Amun.

According to the mythology of that era, Amun was the king of all deities, and he was depicted as a different sort of sphinx. Amun had the head of a ram and the body of a lion. To honor Amun, Pinedjem installed about 100 couchant ram-headed sphinxes at Karnak. Small statuettes of the pharaoh Ramses II, or Ramses the Great, were carved between the paws of the sphinxes. Ramses, whose 67-year rule began in 1279 BC, was one of Egypt's most powerful rulers. The ram sphinxes dedicated to Ramses are about 12 feet (3.6 m) long and 4 feet (1.2 m) wide. They sit on granite pedestals about 17 inches (.43 m) high.

Avenue of the Sphinxes

About four centuries after construction of Pinedjem's sphinxes, another ruler went on a sphinx-building binge at Karnak. Unlike previous rulers, the pharaoh Taharqa was not Egyptian. He was a Nubian from the kingdom of Kush located in a region that is today part of northern Sudan and southern Egypt. The Nubians conquered Egypt in 760 BC, and Taharqa, who ruled from 690 to 664 BC, restored many old temples and built new monuments in Egypt. During this era the god Amun was elevated to the role of Egypt's supreme political authority. This meant Amun granted legitimacy to the kingship and was said to help Taharqa make decisions. To honor Amun, Taharqa commissioned the construction of the avenue of several dozen ram-headed sphinxes to stand guard at the front entrance to Karnak.

By the fourth century BC, however, much of the complex deteriorated due to neglect. When the pharaoh Nectanebo I took the

> # Did You Know?
> In the 1500s BC, over 81,000 people worked at the Karnak temple complex as priests, administrators, huntsmen, and manual laborers. Over 500 gardens, numerous shipping yards, and entire market towns existed within the walls of the complex.

throne around 360 BC he attempted to reverse the decline. Nectanebo ordered the restoration of a 1.7-mile road (2.7 k), called a processional way, that connected the precincts of Mut and Amun-Re. Processional ways were used for solemn ceremonies held by priests and royals during religious events.

Nectanebo lined the processional way, now called the Avenue of Sphinxes, with 1,350 human-headed sphinxes with the bodies of lions. These statues most likely played their traditional role as protectors of the sacred Karnak temples. Although these marvelous statues were buried over time, many have been excavated by archeologists in recent years. Most are missing their heads, but in 2010 the Egyptian government announced a restoration project along the Avenue of Sphinxes. The sphinxes will be pieced together as much as possible from shards found on site, and the avenue will be restored to its former beauty.

Ancient Egyptian Glory

More than 2,000 years elapsed between construction of the Avenue of the Sphinxes and the creation of the Great Sphinx. During those two millennia Egyptian society went through countless changes. For a time, Egypt was the most powerful nation on Earth; later its citizens starved while the county was engulfed in civil wars or ruled by hostile foreigners. The Great Sphinx of Giza remained a constant reminder of ancient Egyptian glory during these long periods of trouble. Its image was preserved in a colossus guarding the pyramids, as statues in holy temples, and as artwork and jewelry possessed by average citizens. Whatever the exact meaning of the sphinx, its mythical association with the gods kept it at the forefront of Egyptian culture for thousands of years.

Chapter 2

The Sphinx in Classical Greece

Around 440 BC the Greek historian Herodotus wrote a nine-volume book called *The Histories*. The book was the earliest ever written that describes ancient Egypt, the pharaohs, and the construction of the pyramids. Herodotus explains that the pyramids were built by the "dragging of great stones from the stone quarries in the Arabian mountains as far as the Nile . . . [by people who] worked in gangs of one hundred thousand each for a period of three months."[11] Describing events that took place more than 2,000 years in the past, Herodotus explains that Khafre, referred to by the Greek name Chephren, built a smaller pyramid next to the Great Pyramid of Khufu. The Greek historian also traced the lineage of a series of pharaohs back hundreds of years. Mysteriously, Herodotus never mentions the Great Sphinx.

Andro-Sphinxes and Flying Snakes

Historians have long wondered why the most renowned classical Greek historian did not describe the Great Sphinx. It is possible Herodotus never actually visited Giza or, if he did, the colossus was mostly buried under sand at the time. Whatever the case may be, Herodotus does make mention of andro-sphinxes, the masculine form of the creature, when describing the exploits of the Pharaoh Amasis II who ruled between 570 and 526 BC:

"[Amasis II] built the gateway of the temple of Minerva at Sais, which is an astonishing work, far surpassing all other buildings of the same kind. . . .

[He] presented to the temple a number of large colossal statues and several prodigious andro-sphinxes ... of a most extraordinary size."[12]

Herodotus does not describe the andro-sphinxes in great detail because his readers surely knew what they looked like. Sphinxes were well known in Greece during the time of Herodotus. The Greeks saw the sphinx as a killer, part of a menagerie of fantastic monsters that many people, including Herodotus, believed were real. As professor of art and archeology William A.P. Childs explains, Herodotus accepts as truth the "accounts of strange beasts that lived on the periphery of the then-known world: flying snakes that invade Egypt from Arabia, giant ants that dig gold in India, and griffins that guard gold."[13]

In The Histories, *written more than 2,000 years after the construction of the Giza pyramids, the Greek historian Herodotus describes their construction. He makes no mention of the Great Sphinx, leading modern historians to speculate that he never actually visited Giza or that the statue was mostly buried by his time.*

Griffins and Gorgons

Griffins are creatures that, like the sphinx, have the body of a lion. Instead of possessing a human head, griffins have the head and wings of an eagle. They are among a large group of sphinx-related leonine, or lionlike, beasts well represented in Greek mythology and art. One creature, the lion-demon, combines a human male body with the head of a lion, the ears of a donkey, and the feet of an eagle or hawk. Ancient Greek legends also speak of lion-dragons with a lion's head, forepaws, and feet and the talons and body of a dragon. The lion-centaur is a sphinxlike mythological beast with a lion's body walking upright and a human male's torso, arms, and head. The creature is sometimes depicted with bird wings on its back.

Many other classical Greek creatures are human-animal hybrids. Perhaps the most terrifying monster is the Gorgon, whose name derived from the Greek word *gorgós*, or "dreadful." The most famous Gorgon, Medusa, is commonly portrayed in Greek artwork as a winged woman with hair made of snakes. She has large, terrible eyes, a wide mouth, short pig tusks, a long protruding tongue, and is sometimes shown with a coarse beard.

She-Monsters

The siren is a bird with a human head or face. The Greek poet Homer described sirens in his epic poem *The Odyssey*, composed around 800 BC. The human-headed birds had irresistibly sweet voices that lured sailors to shipwreck on the rocky shores of the island where they lived. As Homer writes, sirens "enchant all who come near them. If anyone unwarily draws in too close and hears the singing of the Sirens, his wife and children will never welcome him home again, for they sit in a green field and warble him to death with the sweetness of their song. There is a great heap of dead men's bones lying all around, with the flesh still rotting off them."[14]

Greek artists often portrayed sirens with feminine sphinxes that were equally as frightening. According to Greek mythology, the sphinx (sometimes spelled *phix*), was fathered by Typhon, known as the father of all monsters. Typhon had a body reaching halfway to the stars and a hundred dragon heads on each hand. The mother of the Greek sphinx was Echidna, also known as the mother of all monsters. The eighth-century BC poet Hesiod describes Echidna as "half a nymph with glancing eyes and fair cheeks, and half again a huge snake, great and awful, with speckled skin, eating raw flesh beneath the secret parts of the holy earth."[15] Not surprising with such parentage, the sphinx was a hideous demon, a she-monster, half lion, half woman, with the wings of an eagle and the tail of a serpent.

When the sphinxes and sirens were portrayed in Greek artwork, the sirens represented omens of death and the sphinxes were used to transfer the dead to the underworld. Sphinxes were often depicted carrying corpses of young men in their leonine forepaws to the underworld. This gloomy realm, ruled by the god Hades, was where mortals were judged for their past deeds and either blessed or cursed for eternity.

Like the sphinx, the griffin is a hybrid creature. As depicted in this artwork from the 1700s, a griffin has the body of a lion and the head and wings of an eagle.

The Tale of Oedipus

The idea of the female sphinx as a demon of death was incorporated into the mythical tale of Oedipus. The authorship of the story, which emerged around the fifth century BC, is unknown. The tale of Oedipus begins with Laius, the legendary king of Thebes, which was a city-state in Greece (not to be confused with the Egyptian city).

According to the ancient tale, King Laius was married to Queen Jocasta for quite some time, but the couple had no children. Puzzled by the queen's inability to conceive a child, Laius decided to seek counsel from the oracle of Delphi. Delphic oracles were highly respected women who represented the Greek sun god, Apollo. The oracles were thought to have the power to look into the future and offer prophecies to kings and commoners alike. When approached by Laius, the oracle of Delphi went into a trance. Her face flushed, her body trembled, her eyes filled with fire, and she told Laius his wife would soon have a son. She warned him not to celebrate because the boy would someday kill him.

After hearing this dire prediction Laius avoided contact with his wife for many months. However, Jocasta eventually became pregnant and, true to the oracle's prediction, gave birth to a son. Frightened that the child would one day kill him, Laius moved to rid himself of his cursed son. Despite the tears shed by Jocasta, the king took the baby to the wilderness but was unable to kill the innocent infant. Instead the king pinned the baby to the ground by binding his ankles and driving a nail into his foot. Laius left the screaming baby behind with the belief he would either be found by strangers or eaten by wild animals.

The abandoned baby was soon discovered by a wandering shepherd who took him to the city of Corinth. The king and queen of Corinth, named Polybus and Merope, were without children. They adopted the boy, named him Oedipus, and raised him as a prince. Oedipus grew to be a tall, strong, and handsome young man who

Sphinxes and Monsters

The sphinx provided inspiration for a host of creatures depicted in Greek mythology. The Chimera was a monster that combined the leonine body of the sphinx, the head of a goat or ram, and the tail of a snake. The centaur was made from the body of a horse attached to the upper body and head of a man. Although centaurs were known for their drunken antics, they were generally benevolent, known to be smart and helpful to humans. The manticore was a much more frightening creature, with the body of a lion, the head of a man with three rows of razor-sharp teeth, and the tail of a scorpion or dragon that shot out poisonous spines. Manticores were said to devour their victims whole, leaving no clothing or bones behind. In ancient Greece a person who disappeared was said to have been eaten by a manticore—evidence that the creatures were real. A harpy was a terrifying creature with the head of a woman and the body of a large bird. Harpies kidnapped people by snatching them in their talons and flying off. They were said to live in woodlands where they tortured their victims in horrible ways before eating them.

walked with a pronounced limp due to the nail Laius had driven into his foot.

Oedipus was educated, brave, and religious but became troubled when a drunken commoner told him he was not really the son of Polybus. To learn the truth, Oedipus traveled to Delphi to consult with the oracle. She only stated that Oedipus was destined to kill his father. Oedipus did not know his father was Laius who had abandoned him to die. Believing his father was the beloved Polybus, Oedipus decided to leave Corinth hoping to spare the life of Polybus.

The Riddler

Meanwhile, back in Thebes, Laius began ignoring the queen and having relations with a beautiful young man. This angered the deity Hera who was the goddess of women and the protector of marriage. To punish Laius, Hera summoned the sphinx from its home in the mountains of Ethiopia. The sphinx was sent to Thebes to torment the people of the kingdom and devour its subjects. Willis Goth Regier, sphinx expert and director of the University of Illinois Press, describes the evil deeds of the sphinx: "[She] trampled down crops. She charged like a lion. Like an eagle hidden in the sun, she struck suddenly from the sky. She amused herself by conversing with her victims, asking a riddle, playing with her food."[16]

The great riddle of the sphinx was posed to all travelers who passed the monster on the road to Thebes: "What goes on four legs in the morning, two in the afternoon, and three in the evening?"[17] Only the sphinx knew the answer: man. A man crawls on all fours as a baby, walks on two legs as an adult, and walks with a cane, giving him three legs in old age. Dozens of travelers were asked the sphinx's riddle. No one could figure it out, although many died trying.

Laius, whose behavior had brought the sphinx to Thebes, was desperate to rid his kingdom of the monster. He needed to find a solution to the riddle and save his subjects who were being slaughtered at an alarming rate. Laius gathered three soldiers and a slave and left his kingdom by chariot to seek advice from the oracle of Delphi. As Laius drove down the road he encountered Oedipus who was running away from Corinth in order to save Polybus, the man he still believed was his father. Laius and Oedipus did not recognize one another. The old king ordered Oedipus to move aside and let him pass. Oedipus did not realize Laius was a king and, as a pampered young prince, he was unaccustomed to taking orders from anyone. Oedipus refused to move and a battle ensued. Oedipus killed Laius and his soldiers,

Did You Know?

In the fifth century BC, the story of Oedipus and the sphinx formed the basis of renowned plays by the classical Greek authors Aeschylus, Euripides, and Sophocles.

sparing only the life of the slave. The slave ran back to Thebes, and Oedipus limped along behind him.

Kill a Sphinx, Win a Queen

Before Oedipus reached Thebes he encountered travelers on the road who told him the widely held but erroneous belief that Laius was killed by the sphinx. (The travelers were unaware that Oedipus had actually killed Laius, and Oedipus was unaware that the man he had killed was not only the king but his real father.) Oedipus was also informed by the travelers that Jocasta had publically announced she would marry any man who could defeat the evil sphinx that had killed Laius. Oedipus was unaware that Jocasta was his mother. He pondered the situation, as Regier writes: "Raised as a prince—smart, confident, and educated—and uprooted, single, and with little to lose, Oedipus thought it over. He had killed four armed men. Kill one Sphinx to win the queen and a city? How hard could it be?"[18]

Oedipus found his way to the sphinx and gazed upon its beautiful face, flowing black hair, and gold jewelry. The sphinx's leonine body was muscular and taut and its back wings flapped languidly in the breeze. However, the sphinx was surrounded by the remnants of its monstrous crimes. The ground was littered with body parts, blood, crushed bones, and shreds of clothing. Clouds of flies hovered as a ghastly stench of death filled Oedipus's nostrils.

When Oedipus approached, the sphinx pawed the ground with its sharp claws and began to sing the riddle: "What goes on four legs in the morning, two in the afternoon, and three in the evening?" Oedipus knew the answer immediately but remained silent, staring into the mesmerizing face of the sphinx. Finally, he gave the correct answer: man. Upon hearing the correct response the sphinx inexplicably committed suicide by throwing itself off a cliff.

The Thebans celebrated the death of the sphinx. Unaware that they were related to one another, Oedipus and Jocasta were wed. Oedipus was crowned king of Thebes, and the couple bore two sons and two daughters. After many years, a plague of infertility struck

A Greek Dilemma

Classical Greek author Aeschylus wrote several plays about the sphinx, Oedipus, and Thebes, which have been lost over the centuries. However, modern historians have found scenes depicted on vases and cups believed to be from these plays. From these depictions, historians have constructed a different version of the Oedipus story. This tale concerns a character with the tongue-twisting name Papposilenus who was depicted wearing tights, a panther skin, and a headband. When encountering the sphinx, Papposilenus refused to answer its riddle, instead proposing a riddle of his own. He held up a bird in his right hand and asked the sphinx if it is dead or alive. If the sphinx said dead, Papposilenus let the bird fly away to prove her wrong. If the sphinx said alive, he choked the bird to death. While this does not sound like much of a riddle to modern ears, the Greeks were fond of this sort of problem. They called it a dilemma, a problem that has two answers, neither of which is practical or acceptable.

Thebes. Women could not have children, crops would not grow, and the kingdom was threatened with mass starvation. Oedipus believed he could end the plague if only the oracle of Delphi would provide him with a solution. He sent Jocasta's brother to Delphi for answers. The brother returned to Oedipus and told him that the plague would end if the murderer of Laius were found and either killed or expelled from Thebes.

Oedipus consulted with a prophet named Tiresias for guidance. He warned him not to pursue Laius's killer. After an argument with Oedipus, Tiresias finally told him the truth. He was the son of Laius and Jocasta and he had killed his true father. When the queen heard this news, she hung herself. Oedipus discovered her body, took a brooch from Jocasta's gown, and gouged his own eyes out with the pin. In the following years, Oedipus wandered blindly through Greece until his death many years later.

Offerings and Guardians

The tale of Oedipus, the sphinx, and its riddle was one of the most popular stories of fifth-century Greece. The story was also a popular subject for artists. The episode of the sphinx meeting Oedipus on the road to Thebes was depicted countless times on vases and other ceramic works. A standard scene shows Oedipus sitting before the sphinx, which is standing on a column. A crowd of seated Thebans watches the riddle contest.

Over time the sphinx came to be seen as a more positive symbol than its traditional portrayal in Greek lore. Some classical Greeks viewed the creature as the ancient Egyptians had, as a benefactor and protector. This belief was represented by statues of the sphinx used as votive offerings in temples. Votive offerings are objects that are left at sacred sites by those who wish to gain favor from gods, goddesses, or other supernatural forces. One of the most stunning sphinx votives was created for Delphi, the home of the oracle of Apollo featured in the Oedipus story. The sphinx was created by the people of the wealthy land of Naxos, a Greek island in the Aegean Sea.

The Sphinx of Naxos, carved around 560 BC, is 7.2 feet (2.2 m) high and 4.4 feet (1.35 m) long. The white marble statue once sat atop a huge column, 33 feet (10 m) high. From this perch the sphinx served as a guardian of the shrine of Delphi. The Delphi Archaeological Museum, where the sphinx is now displayed, offers a description of the fantastic statue:

> The sphinx (woman-lion-bird) sits flat on its haunches, its forelegs fully extended. The chest is carved with a . . . breastplate of feathers; the wings extensively detailed with

Did You Know?

While the sphinx throws itself off a wall in the classic telling of the Greek tale, in a later version it is killed by Oedipus or dies of shock when its riddle is correctly answered.

longer, more elaborate versions of the same. The head, set on a long neck, faces straight ahead. The long, narrow face exhibits triangular-shaped eyes, a flatish mouth and a receding chin. The hair is treated with [decorative edging] around the forehead and regular, continuous rows of beads on the crown of the head, held in place by a [headband] tied at the back. . . . [The] mass of hair, beaded only along the edges, follows the curve of the back of the neck.[19]

The Naxian sphinx dominated the Delphic shrine for hundreds of years. An inscription carved into the base of the column in 328 BC says *P*R*O*M*A*N*T*E*I*A. Experts say this means that the sphinx gave Naxians priority in consulting the Delphic oracle.

Greek art expert John J. Herrmann explains the symbolism of the sphinx of Delphi as it relates to the Oedipus story: "The riddle becomes a metaphor for the obscure but enlightening utterances of the [oracles]. . . . There is [a warning aspect] as well; those who cannot seriously consider or interpret such ambiguous pronouncements should advance no further."[20] In this way, the Naxian sphinx kept the general public from approaching the Delphic oracles. Those who did consult the prophets could expect prophecies in the form of word puzzles rather than direct answers.

Athena and the Sphinx

The sphinx at Delphi was one of many that were placed at important sites throughout the Greek lands. Similar statues have been found in the ancient city of Cyrene in modern Libya and the islands of Paros and Delos in Greece. An image of the sphinx was also incorporated into a colossal statue called Athena Parthenos. The colossus was created around 440 BC by the sculptor Phidias and towered over the Parthenon, one of the most important buildings in the city of Athens.

Sphinx images appeared in artwork throughout ancient Greece. A likeness of the sphinx was prominent on the helmet of a large statue of Athena Parthenos (pictured in an engraving), which once stood in the Parthenon in Athens.

MINERVE DU PARTHENON

Athena Parthenos was created to honor Athena, the preeminent goddess of classical Athens. According to mythology, Athena sprang fully grown and fully armed from the head of her father, Zeus, who was the king of all gods. Athena was credited with inventing the flute, the plow, and the chariot. She was worshipped as the goddess of wisdom, weaving, textiles, justice, strength, and heroes. The goddess was believed to have founded the city of Athens which was named for her. Athena Parthenos was 40 feet (12 m) high and a wonder of ancient sculpture. It was described by the historian Pausanias in the second century BC:

> The statue itself is made of ivory, silver and gold. On the middle of her helmet is placed a likeness of the Sphinx . . . and on either side of the helmet are griffins in relief. . . . The statue of Athena is upright, with a tunic reaching to the feet, and on her breast the head of Medusa is worked in ivory. She holds a statue of Victory about four cubits (about 6 feet or 2m) high, and in the other hand a spear; at her feet lies a shield and near the spear is a serpent.[21]

Historians believe the statue was built with a wooden core covered with bronze plates that formed Athena's features. Plates representing the goddess's robe, helmet, and other features were covered with about 2,500 pounds (1,100 kg) of gold while Athena's face and arms were ivory. Other features were cast from silver. The sphinx prominently featured on Athena's helmet undoubtedly stood for protection and leonine strength and watchfulness. However, according to ancient written reports, the gold plating was stripped from the statue in the late third century BC by Lachares, a tyrant who ruled Athens and plundered the city's wealth. While descriptions of Athena Parthenos remain, and replicas have been created, the original colossus was believed to have been destroyed in a fire around the fifth century AD.

A Symbol with Many Meanings

The powerful rulers of Greece perceived the sphinx as a magical symbol meant to ward off evil or deflect misfortune. Average citizens sought to make use of this power after death when their souls entered the underworld. For this reason statues and carved images of sphinxes appeared on thousands of tombstones and monuments in ancient Greece. In this form, the creature was not a passive protector but a force meant to keep evil at bay.

An inscription on a stela decorated with a sphinx in an ancient Greek graveyard addresses the mythical monster as the Dog of Hades and asks its own riddle: "Dog of Hades, whom do you . . . watch over, sitting over the dead?" An inscription from another stela provides an answer: "I protect the chapel of the tomb. I guard thy sepulchral chamber. I ward off the intruding stranger. I hurl thy foes to the ground."[22]

The classical era ended in 146 BC when Greece was overrun by the Romans, who also went on to conquer Egypt in 30 BC. During the centuries that the Romans ruled Egypt, they used the sphinx as a symbol of the sun and an emblem of their power. Coins minted by Roman rulers including Caligula, Claudius, and Hadrian, featured the winged female sphinx of Greek origins. Christianity emerged as an important religion during the Roman era, and early Christians might also have viewed the sphinx as a symbol of the sun. Christian graves were decorated with sphinxes now believed to have symbolized the divine light of Jesus.

Whatever the era, the sphinx was many things to many people. As a strangler, a challenger, a protector, and a divine light, people molded the image of the sphinx to fit their needs. For Oedipus the riddle of the sphinx had only one answer. For all others, the Greek sphinx posed many questions and spawned countless stories. The sphinx's riddles have been forever woven into the fabric of human culture.

Did You Know?

One of the oldest books about demons, *The Testament of Solomon*, written in the fourth century AD, warns that demons can be "sphinx-faced," or have facial features similar to the sphinx.

Chapter 3

Sphinxes in the Modern Era

The modern era is a period of history that began in the 1500s and is marked by the rise in power of European and other Western nations. From the beginning of the modern era, the Great Sphinx of Giza and tales of the Greek sphinx inspired Western poets, artists, scholars, and philosophers.

Knowledge of the Great Sphinx first reached Europe in the fourteenth century when travelers from France, Italy, and elsewhere began visiting Egypt in large numbers. In the centuries that followed, countless European merchants traveled to Egypt on a regular basis returning home with sphinx statues, jewelry, and artwork plundered from ancient ruins. These items were valued by wealthy Europeans who paid high prices for them.

Many European tourists and scholars who visited Egypt wrote books about their travels. In 1581 Italian physician and botanist Prospero Alpini visited Giza to gaze in wonder at the pyramids and the Great Sphinx. Several years later he described the sphinx: "It presents an immense and very large face, looking toward Cairo and sculpted in every way with great competency. That is to say, its chin, its mouth, its nose, its eyes, its brow and its ears seem to be cut with profound knowledge of the art of sculpture."[23]

A few years after Alpini's visit, the French naturalist Pierre Bulon called the sphinx "a sculpted monster which is a virgin in front and has the body of a lion."[24] Bulon also mentioned that he did not want to dwell too long on a description of the sphinx because so much had already been written about it.

Renaissance Sphinxes

The Egyptian art craze coincided with a rebirth of the arts in Italy called the Renaissance. During the Renaissance, which lasted from the fourteenth to the sixteenth centuries, renowned artists like Donatello, Leonardo da Vinci, and Michelangelo produced some of the world's most valuable artwork. The Renaissance was based on a revival of artistic, philosophical, and scientific knowledge from classical Greece and ancient Egypt. Inspired by religious beliefs of the past, artists mixed Greek and Egyptian imagery with biblical themes to produce unique Renaissance artwork.

Sphinxes adorn both sides of the throne on which a seated Virgin Mary holds the baby Jesus. Beside them, in this fifteenth-century sculpture by the artist Donatello, are Saint Francis and Saint Anthony.

Around 1450 the artist Donatello sculpted the *Madonna and Child*, a statue that portrays the Virgin Mary sitting on a throne with the baby Jesus on her lap. The throne is supported by two sphinxes. In the early twentieth century, Scottish nobleman and art historian David Lindsay, also known as Lord Balcarres, described the mood created by the Egyptian symbols in Donatello's sculpture:

> The Virgin herself is of unequalled solemnity, while her young and gracious face, exquisite in expression and contour, is full of queenly beauty. But there is still an atmosphere of mystery, an enigmatic aloofness in spite of the warm human sentiment. The Sphinx's faces, with all their traditions of secrecy, contribute their share to the cryptic environment.[25]

The sphinxes in Donatello's sculpture were meant to represent the wisdom of the goddess Athena. However, the Renaissance sphinx was sometimes used to symbolize ignorance. This was seen in the drawing *Allegory of Vice and Virtue* created around 1490 by Italian painter Andrea Mantegna. The drawing shows two female sphinxes supporting a globe, which represents the world. Sitting atop the globe, dominating humanity, a nude, obese female named Ignorance wears a crown. Other figures in the drawing represent Error, Lust, Envy, and Greed. While the expressions of the sphinxes exhibit unhappiness, they support a world ruled by Ignorance.

The French Sphinx

Mantegna's winged female sphinxes were modeled on the Greek tradition. The sphinx took on a new form near the end of the fifteenth century with the discovery in Rome of a cave filled with wall paintings, or frescos, some of which featured highly stylized sphinxes. Renaissance scholars identified the cave as part of a renowned villa called Domus Aurea (Golden House or Golden Palace), occupied by the Roman ruler Nero in the first century AD. Nero's villa was called the Golden Palace because the ceilings were overlaid in gold leaf and embedded with gems and rare seashells. After Nero's suicide in AD 68, the Golden Palace was seen as an embarrassing reminder of Nero's tyrannical rule. The sumptuous villa was buried and used as a construction site by the emperor's successor.

When the Golden Palace was accidentally rediscovered 15 centuries later the frescoes were faded but remained intact. They showed images of strange beasts that melded bird wings, fish tails, animal bodies, and human faces. According to renowned author Robert Penn Warren, these images were in an unusual style, "strange and absurd, suggesting an otherness in preposterous form and effecting in the viewer feelings of fascination, amusement, uneasiness, fear."[26] This bizarre style of depicting creatures with exaggerated features in great detail came to be known as grotesque.

Renaissance artists Michelangelo, Raphael, and others descended into the Golden Palace using knotted ropes as ladders. They studied the ancient Roman art and carved their names into the walls. Inspired by the images, the Renaissance artists began creating beastly creatures in the grotesque style.

Artists of the era depicted the grotesque sphinx as a fantastic flying creature with a small body and large head, torso, and woman's breasts. The long flowing hair was depicted in great detail, and the creature was often shown wearing pearl necklaces, earrings, and other jewelry. This grotesque sphinx was also called the French sphinx because it was extremely popular in France in the seventeenth and eighteenth centuries. As French Egyptologist Nicolas Grimal explains, during this era, "there was a revival of exotic architecture, and Egyptianizing sphinxes jostled with stone or wooden pyramids in European gardens."[27]

While artists and sculptors created French sphinx art, ancient sphinxes were also in great demand. Statues dating back to the third

A carved Egyptian sphinx, one of a pair that graces the banks of the Neva River at Saint Petersburg in Russia, is one of the oldest sphinxes found outside of Egypt. The pair is believed to have been carved around 1500 BC.

millennium BC were brought to European capitals and placed in palace gardens and public squares in France, Austria, Germany, Poland, Spain, and elsewhere. The trend continued into the nineteenth century, and some of the oldest sphinxes outside Egypt are in the unlikely location of St. Petersburg, Russia. A pair of huge Egyptian sphinxes, carved around 1500 BC, were placed along the banks of the Neva River in 1820. According to the website English Russia, these are the northernmost sphinxes in the world, and St. Petersburg is "probably the only place in the world where you can see ... Egyptian, 3500 year old sphinxes covered with snow."[28]

A Symbol of Many Things

While sphinx art has been extremely popular over the centuries, the creature has also been well represented in literature. Authors have used the sphinx as a symbol of mystery, wisdom, stupidity, and horror.

British philosopher, statesman, and scientist Francis Bacon saw the sphinx as a representation of science. In his 1619 book *Wisdom of the Ancients* Bacon wrote that the sphinx's bright face and imagined voice symbolized the pleasing verbal exchange of ideas between scientists. Using Elizabethan English spellings, Bacon writes that the wings of the sphinx represent science because "inventions do passe and flie from one to another." Science is also signified by the sharp, hooked talons on the feet of the sphinx "because the [accepted truths] and arguments of Science do so fasten upon the mind."[29]

Bacon goes on to explain that as long as people are unable to solve the sphinxlike riddles of nature, the gods will be content. But once scientists understand the inner workings of nature, the gods will assault minds with riddles even more difficult than the riddle once posed by the sphinx to Oedipus.

The colossus remained a terrible monster in the minds of many. In the modern era, Egyptians often referred to the Great Sphinx using the Arabic words *Abu'l Hol*, which translates to "Father of Terror." Egyptologist Christiane Zivie-Coche speculates about how this designation came to be: "The strange sight of a head emerging from the sand could not have failed to inspire fear, given that all sorts of maleficent genies and ghouls were said to roam the neighborhood."[30]

During the Renaissance the sphinx was portrayed by Italian poet Torquato Tasso as a hideously horrible creature. In 1581 Tasso published *Jerusalem Delivered* in which he describes the sphinx spewing forth from hell in the company of thousands of Gorgons, centaurs, and Harpies. Regier comments on the poem: "The bloodthirsty Sphinx has been seen in bad company, a monster among monsters."[31]

In 1820 British poet Percy Bysshe Shelley also placed the sphinx in bad company in the four-act play *Prometheus Unbound*. In Greek mythology Prometheus is best known as the god who stole fire from Zeus and gave it to mortals. As punishment, Zeus chained Prometheus to a rock and had an eagle eat his liver every day, having it grow back so the process was repeated forever. *Prometheus Unbound* describes the god's release from captivity. However, as Prometheus is about to be freed, Mercury arrives to threaten new tortures and calls forth the sphinx, along with a Gorgon, a Chimera, and a Geryon. Nothing could be more horrendous than this combination of creatures. A Chimera is a fire-breathing female monster with the body of a lion, a goat head in the center of her spine, and a tail that ends with a snake's head. A Geryron is a giant with a human face, six feet, six hands, and wings. As Mercury calls out to Prometheus:

> [Gnash] beside the streams of fire and wail,
>
> Your foodless teeth. Geryon, arise! and Gorgon, Chimera,
>   and thou Sphinx, subtlest of fiends,
>
> Who ministered to Thebes Heaven's poisoned wine,
>
> Unnatural love, and more unnatural hate.[32]

The Devourer

French painter Gustave Moreau created a painting called *Oedipus and the Sphinx* in 1864. He provided commentary to the Salon art exhibition to explain the meaning of the painting.

The painter envisages man, having arrived at [a] grave and severe hour of life, finding himself in the presence of the eternal enigma [the sphinx]. It presses and grasps him with its terrible claws. But the traveler [Oedipus], proud and calm in his moral force, gazes upon it without trembling. It is the earthly Chimera, vile like matter, attractive like it, represented by this charming head of a woman, with wings . . . promising the ideal and the body of the monster, of the devourer who rips apart and destroys.

Quoted in Scott C. Allan, "Interrogating Gustave Moreau's Sphinx: Myth as Artistic Metaphor in the 1864 Salon," Nineteenth-Century Art Worldwide, 2010. www.19thc-artworldwide.org.

Three Paintings

Shelley was part of a literary and artistic movement known as Romanticism, which flourished from the late 1700s until the mid-1800s. Romantics created emotional works that inspired feelings of awe, foreboding, dreamlike wonder, sadness, and horror. Romance artists often created paintings of ancient ruins to evoke notions of haunted, lost worlds and glum thoughts about death and decay. As a symbol of mystery, melancholy, and terror, the sphinx in its many forms embodied Romantic values like few other ancient monsters.

The sphinx was so fascinating to French painter Jean-Auguste-Dominique Ingres that he created three versions of the Oedipus riddle scene over the course of his career. The first, created in 1808 when the painter was 28 years old, is called *Oedipus and the Sphinx*.

The painting shows Oedipus, naked, in profile, facing the Sphinx which is standing in the shadows of a cave. He points to himself with his right hand and points to the sphinx with his left hand, finger upraised as if to tickle the monster. Oedipus is standing on one foot, resting his other on a rock before the sphinx, and is holding two spears, perhaps referring to the two, three, and four legs of the riddle. At the bottom of the painting, the ground is littered with human bones and a disembodied foot left by travelers who failed to answer the riddle correctly. Oedipus is answering the sphinx with a knowledgeable look on his face. In 1825 Ingres returned to the painting, made the sphinx bigger, and added a figure in the background of a terrified man running away.

In 1864 Ingres created another version of *Oedipus and the Sphinx*. In this version the sphinx is more monstrous but depicted with human breasts. Oedipus exhibits a calm demeanor while the sphinx looks away with an expression of pained horror, perhaps understanding its imminent suicide. This work, created when Ingres was 85, is more refined but symbolizes the painter's looming death. Ingres signed his name roughly on a rock in the foreground along with the date and his age. It was one of his last major works before his death in 1867.

The Eternal Enigma

Ingres influenced another French painter, Gustave Moreau, who also created a painting called *Oedipus and the Sphinx*. Unlike Ingres's sphinx, perched upon a rock, the creature in Moreau's 1864 painting is clinging to the standing Oedipus like a cat climbing up a tree. The front paws of the sphinx cling to a sash around Oedipus's body and

In one version of Oedipus and the Sphinx *painted by French artist Jean-Auguste-Dominique Ingres Oedipus looks directly into the face of the sphinx as he correctly answers its riddle. Scattered at the prince's feet are the remains of travelers who failed to answer the sphinx's deadly riddle.*

its back paws are pressed against his thighs. Moreau's sphinx is face-to-face with its adversary, Oedipus, and its eyes are locked onto his. The face of the sphinx is beautiful but body parts are strewn on the ground, a grisly reminder of its monstrousness.

When Moreau's sphinx was presented at the prestigious Salon art show in Paris it was hailed by critics as a work of both artistic achievement and profound symbolism. Critics stated that by showing the sphinx clutching to Oedipus, Moreau was poetically illustrating the struggle between the idealized human spirit and the corrupting influences of sensual pleasure, materialism, and vice.

Continued Transformation

The American painter Elihu Vedder did not see the sphinx as a mythological Greek monster but as an ancient Egyptian messenger. His 1863 painting *The Questioner of the Sphinx* portrays the head of the great Egyptian sphinx barely emerged from the surrounding sand. A dark figure crouches before the colossus pressing his ear to the lips of the ancient sage. The bleak landscape appears to be an apocalyptic wasteland with ruins of columns and possibly the pyramids. Vedder returned to this theme 12 years later with *Listening to the Sphinx*. In this painting a very old bearded man listens to the sphinx, possibly in hope of finding the answer to eternal life.

In twentieth century art, the sphinx continued to transform as the world changed. The European-schooled American painter John Singer Sargent is widely known for his portraits of the rich and famous. He was among the first artists, however, to portray the sphinx in a light-hearted manner. *Sphinx and the Chimera* was one of Sargent's last paintings, created for the rotunda at the Boston Museum of Fine Art a few years before his death in 1925. The work shows an updated version of the Great Sphinx with a handsome upturned face. The sphinx gazes lovingly into the eyes of a nude, flying Chimera. The

Chimera in Sargent's work is far different from the traditional monster. This creature is a whimsical beauty with a woman's body and head and the elaborately painted wings of a bird. By the time this mural was created, the term "chimera" was used to mean a foolish fantasy, and this angel-like creature seems to be part of the sphinx's daydream.

Perhaps no artist has painted more unusual sphinxes than Salvador Dalí. As a twentieth-century master of the surrealist style, Dalí painted everyday objects in a bizarre manner, placed in settings that were out of context. For example, his famous painting *The Persistence of Memory* shows pocket watches that seem to have melted and are

An old man presses his ear to the lips of the Great Sphinx, perhaps hoping to hear the secret to eternal life. The painter, American artist Elihu Vedder, saw the sphinx as an ancient messenger rather than as a mythological monster.

draped over a tree branch and a table's edge. When Dalí chose to portray the sphinx in several paintings, the images were disturbing and fraught with meaning. In the 1931 *Remorse or Sunken Sphinx*, the sphinx is portrayed as a real woman, half buried in the sand. She has no lion body but is shown from behind with her hand to her head. She seems to be weeping with regret.

In Dalí's *Three Sphinxes of Bikini* three heads protrude from the ground, one in the foreground, the others receding into the distance. Dalí painted this a year after the US Navy tested an atom bomb on the Bikini atoll in the Pacific. Instead of hair, Dalí's sphinx heads consist of billowing smoke resembling the mushroom cloud created by the nuclear explosion.

A Comic Book Superhero

Dalí used the sphinx to illustrate pain, remorse, and fear, but the most frightening aspects of the image have been diluted in the past century. Since the early 1990s the sphinx has appeared in puzzles, computer games, postage stamps, money, slot machines, and on fortune-telling tarot cards. There are Sphinx brand bicycles, coffees, teas, and cigarettes. Throughout the world, hotels, bars, restaurants, and casinos bear the sphinx's name or likeness. The fraternal organization known as the Freemasons uses the sphinx as a decoration for documents and Masonic temples. Several species of animals have been named after the sphinx, including the sphinx monkey, the sphinx fruit bat, and the sphinx moth. Dozens of mountain peaks and geological outcroppings from the Swiss Alps to Montana are named Sphinx. And like any good mythical monster, the sphinx has found a special place in comic books.

In 1977 the sphinx appeared as a mutant monster Anath-Na Mut in Marvel Comics. This indestructible, animated stone creature could tap into ancient Egyptian magic, fly through the air, read minds, and overpower its enemies with superhuman strength. This

> **Did You Know?**
>
> The summit of the striking Sphinx Mountain in the Madison Range of Montana rises 10,876 feet (3,315 m) above sea level.

creature was revived in 1989 as part of a superhero team called New Warriors. Sphinxes have also appeared in many guises in countless Japanese comics, or manga.

The sphinx remains an object of fascination and wonderment in the twenty-first century. As the ultimate "symbol of symbols,"[33] according to Regier, the icon of the sphinx has come to represent doubt, curses, good luck, bad luck, boredom, anguish, eternity, fame, silence, memory, menace, and a host of other conditions. Wherever the sphinx is found, the ancient creature of the desert has become an instantly recognizable part of modern culture.

Chapter 4

Ancient Monument, Modern Theories

The majority of Egyptologists and archeologists believe ancient Egyptian civilization came into existence around 3050 BC. At that time, a powerful Egyptian prince named Narmer united dozens of small villages along the Nile into a single nation. Over the centuries, this nation grew, and by 2050 BC, it had evolved into the richest nation on Earth. The pharaohs of this period, known as the Old Kingdom, used their wealth to build the pyramids of Giza and the Great Sphinx. While many details about the construction of these monuments remain a mystery, the Egyptians left extensive written records about hundreds of other aspects of their civilization, religion, and government. These records have allowed historians to create a widely accepted picture of the Old Kingdom and a timeline concerning significant events such as the creation of the Great Sphinx.

Deciphering ancient history involves some guesswork, and like most historical interpretations, established theories about the Great Sphinx cannot be proved with complete certainty. As a result, doubts about the sphinx's origins and age have sparked debate among amateur historians and scientists, along with those who believe in the supernatural. Some who challenge mainstream beliefs about the Great Sphinx are more believable than others. Whatever the case, unconventional theories persist regarding the creators of the sphinx and the age of the ancient colossus.

The Hall of Records

The psychic Edgar Cayce was one of the first people to put forth alternative theories about the Great Sphinx in the twentieth century. Cayce made his living predicting the future, claiming to heal sick people through psychic means and making pronouncements about events in the long distant past. Followers said Cayce predicted the 1929 Great Depression several years before it occurred. The public was fascinated by Cayce's apparently supernatural abilities, and in the 1920s and 1930s he was as famous as celebrity movie stars, politicians, and athletes.

Despite the many written records that document the life and culture of ancient Egypt, few details are known about the construction of the Great Sphinx. Here, an artist imagines what the work site might have looked like.

When he performed what he called "life readings," Cayce entered a deep trance, which earned him the name the "Sleeping Prophet." During his trance experiences, Cayce claimed to visit ancient Egypt,

ancient Greece, and other lands. During one such event in October 1933, Cayce said he mentally traveled to the Great Sphinx and found a secret sealed room called the Hall of Records located under the paws of the colossus.

In the following years Cayce often spoke of the Hall of Records. He said documents within the room revealed to him that the Great Sphinx was built in 10,500 BC by a king named Araaraat. The monument was a symbol representing the spiritual relationship between animals and humans. According to Cayce, the builders of the sphinx hailed from the lost continent of Atlantis, a mythical land in the Atlantic Ocean populated by a race of superintelligent beings around 15,000 years ago. Cayce claimed that he had lived in Atlantis in a past life.

While no facts support the existence of Atlantis, believers say the mythical island was destroyed by volcanoes and tsunamis. It supposedly disappeared beneath the sea, killing most of its inhabitants. However, some Atlanteans were said to have escaped the calamity and moved to North Africa, where they founded a civilization that became ancient Egypt.

A New Generation of Investigators

Cayce died in 1945, but he still has thousands of followers throughout the world who fervently believe his pronouncements about the Hall of Records and the Great Sphinx despite a lack of evidence for either and the fact that he never actually traveled to Egypt. Cayce made hundreds of predictions that never came true, including one that stated the Hall of Records would be discovered in 1998. Upon that discovery, Cayce said the history of the earth would be revealed, humanity would be moved into a new era of prosperity, and the events would coincide with the Second Coming of Christ.

Despite Cayce's many failed prophecies and questionable historical facts, the notion that the Sphinx is far older than commonly

Wind, Sand, Rain, and Erosion

The core, or body, of the sphinx is carved from limestone, a stone that exhibits different wear patterns depending on the source of the erosion. The British writer Colin Wilson describes wind, sand, and rain erosion and their effects on the Great Sphinx:

> Limestone is a sedimentary rock, made of particles [compressed] together; and, as everyone knows, such rocks come in strata, like a layer cake. When wind-blown sand hits the side of the layer cake, the softer layers are worn away, while the harder layers stick out above and below them. The result is a series of parallel layers, with a profile of humps and hollows like the profile of a club sandwich.
>
> When a rock face is eroded by rain water, the effect is totally different. The rain runs down in streams, and cuts vertical channels into the rock. The softer rock is still eroded more deeply than the harder, but the effect is quite distinct from wind-weathering—it can look like a series of bumps, not unlike a row of naked buttocks. [Research teams] agreed that both the body of the Sphinx and the Sphinx enclosure showed this type of weathering, not the smoother effect of wind-weathering.

Colin Wilson, *From Atlantis to the Sphinx*. New York: Fromm, 1996, pp. 38–39.

believed and that it has a secret chamber caught on with the public. In the decades after Cayce's death, a new generation of investigators began examining the age of the sphinx. Some used scientific tests and educated observations to back the theory that the sphinx was built around 12,500 years ago by a civilization that was destroyed in a mysterious catastrophe. Others searched for secret chambers in or around the sphinx, hoping to find ancient manuscripts that might prove their theories.

Wind and Rain Erosion

Robert Schoch, a professor and geologist at Boston University, is among those who have employed scientific methods in an effort to prove that the Great Sphinx is much older than commonly believed. Schoch is a traditionally trained scientist with an interest in paranormal phenomena. He was initially skeptical about challenging mainstream thought concerning the age of the sphinx, assuming the Egyptologists were correct in their dating. However, after traveling to Egypt in 1990 to conduct geological research on the sphinx, Schoch discovered evidence that he believed proved the sphinx to be much older than commonly believed. According to Schoch: "On the body of the Sphinx, and on the walls of the Sphinx Enclosure (the pit or hollow remaining after the Sphinx's body was carved from the bedrock), I found heavy [erosion] that I concluded could only have been caused by rainfall and water runoff."[34] Erosion, or the gradual wearing away of the stone, can be caused by rain, as Schoch says, or by wind and blowing sand. Whether the sphinx was eroded by wind or rain is at the center of the debate concerning the age of the colossus.

The sphinx is located in the Sahara Desert, a region that receives less than 1 inch (2.5 cm) of rainfall annually. This weather pattern has been consistent for the past 5,000 years. (Egyptians have long survived on the waters of the Nile which are replenished by heavy rains and mountain snows that fall in central Africa.) Little water erosion of any type has occurred on the pyramids of Giza, which are known to have been built around 2500 BC. The pyramids, located about 1,700 feet (518 m) from the sphinx, are pitted from wind and blowing sand, which create erosion patterns markedly different than those caused by water.

Did You Know?

Psychic Edgar Cayce claimed that when the Great Sphinx was constructed 12,000 years ago, human beings had tails.

The story becomes more complex when theories of historical weather patterns in northern Egypt are taken into account. Those who have studied the climate in ancient Egypt conclude that the region had significant rainfall from about 10,000 to 5000 BC. During this time the Sahara was a green grassland, or savanna. While the major rainfall ended around 5000 BC, a period of sporadic but torrential rains lasted from about 4000 to 3000 BC, an era known as the Predynastic Period.

The rains stopped around the time the first written records from ancient Egypt were produced. After this period, known as the Early Dynastic Period, the region became a desert as rain stopped falling in any significant quantities.

Carved Before 5000 BC?

By studying the erosion patterns on the body of the sphinx and reading ancient climate data, Schoch concluded that the sphinx is older

Most researchers believe the Great Sphinx was built around 2550 BC, but some say it was erected much earlier, at a time when rain in the area was plentiful. The Nile River, pictured, is replenished seasonally by heavy rains and mountain snows originating in central Africa.

than commonly believed. To further test his theory, he conducted a test called a seismic study. To do so, he pressed a steel plate against the rock under the sphinx's head and pounded it with a sledgehammer. Using a special sound wave–measuring device, he discovered information about the depth of rain erosion upon the rock. According to Schoch, "When I analyzed the data, I found that the extraordinary depth of subsurface weathering supported my conclusion that the core-body of the Sphinx must date back to 5000 BC or earlier."[35]

The new estimate of the sphinx's age led Schoch to propose an answer to the riddle of the sphinx's head. People have long wondered why the head on the statue is smaller and out of proportion with the rest of the body. Schoch concluded that 8,000 years ago the head of the sphinx was much larger and carved with the face of a lion. When the original details eroded, it was re-carved with the face of Khafre or another pharaoh sometime around 2550 BC. If true, it would explain the disproportioned head.

The seismic test revealed another surprise, according to Schoch. He says he found evidence that a room might exist under the sphinx's left paw. Schoch was unaware at the time of Cayce's predictions about a Hall of Records. However, one of his partners during the research, amateur Egyptologist John Anthony West, has repeatedly stated over the decades that the room was the secret chamber envisioned by Cayce. Egyptian authorities will not allow excavation in this area to prove or disprove the existence of a room. Whatever the case, West wrote articles and books that proclaimed the sphinx was created 12,500 years ago by Atlanteans, and the legendary Hall of Records contains texts that explain how the pyramids were built.

Grave Implications

Schoch presented his findings at the annual meeting of the Geological Society of America in San Diego in 1991. A number of geologists agreed with the concept, and the 9,000-year-old sphinx theory gained widespread recognition in 1993. At that time NBC television aired the hour-long documentary *Mystery of the Sphinx*, filmed by Schoch and West and financed by an organization founded by Cayce called Association for Research and Enlightenment. The TV program, seen by an estimated 30 million people, features Schoch presenting evidence to back his erosion theory while West discusses the Atlantis connection. During the program West made this startling pronouncement:

> If the single fact of the water erosion of the Sphinx could be confirmed, it would in itself overthrow all accepted chronologies of the history of civilization; it would force a drastic re-evaluation of the assumption of "progress"—the assumption upon which the whole of modern education is based. It would be difficult to find a single, simple question with graver implications.[36]

West implies that if the sphinx had been built by a mysteriously vanished human society in 7000 or 10,000 BC, the known chronology of world civilization would be called into question. It would mean that long ago, people with technological and organizational capabilities were advanced enough to carve the Sphinx and possibly the temples that have been excavated nearby.

American Hallucinations

Skeptics point out that no traces have been found of extremely ancient civilizations advanced enough to carve a colossus like the sphinx, although Schoch notes that well-esbablished cities already existed in Palestine and Turkey by about 7000 BC. Schoch adds: "Quite possibly other cultural remains are, for the most part, buried deep under the Nile alluvium [soil and sand]. In addition, rises in sea level since 10,000 or 15,000 years ago may have submerged vast expanses along the Mediterranean coast inhabited by early cultures."[37]

Schoch was embarrassed by the Atlantean connection put forth by West because it detracted from his science-based conclusions. Fur-

Ancient Advanced Cultures

Geologist Robert Schoch defends his theory that the sphinx was created around 7000 BC or even later by pointing out that advanced cultures existed outside of Egypt at that time:

[In Turkey] Catal Hüyük, a city built of mud bricks and timber, dates back to at least the late–Seventh Millennium B.C. This was no primitive settlement, however; rather, the known remains demonstrate a sophistication and opulence previously unimagined by archaeologists for such a remote period in time. The inhabitants built elaborate houses and shrines, covered walls with paintings and reliefs, and apparently had a rich and complex symbolic and religious tradition.

Jericho [in Palestine] dates back to the Ninth Millennium B.C. and the city-site included a massive stone wall and tower, and a ditch cut in the bedrock—all dating from 8000 B.C. The remains of the stone wall are at least six and one-half feet (2 meters) thick and still stand in places twenty feet (6 meters) high (nobody knows how high it was originally). . . . Inside the wall are the remains of a stone tower thirty feet (9.1 meters) in diameter, the ruins of this structure still standing thirty feet (9.1 meters) high. . . . This construction has been compared favorably to the towers seen on the great medieval castles of Europe.

Robert M. Schoch, "Redating the Great Sphinx of Giza," *Circular Times*, 2009. www.robertschoch.net.

ther research was halted when West and Schoch were banned from the sphinx site by the former head of Egypt's Supreme Council of Antiquities, Zahi Hawass, after their documentary aired. Hawass, a world-renowned Egyptologist, was angered by the theory that linked the sphinx to Atlantis, calling the theory "American hallucinations" and stating "there is no scientific base for any of this. We have older monuments in the same area. They definitely weren't built by men from Atlantis. It's nonsense and we won't allow our monuments to be exploited for personal enrichment. The Sphinx is the soul of Egypt."[38]

Sphinx Island

Despite the best efforts of Hawass, since the mid-1990s, the theory of a Predynastic Sphinx has been studied and discussed in dozens of books, articles, and websites. Mainstream Egyptologists continue to dispute this idea while others, such as Robert Temple, have modified it. Temple has worked as a science writer for mainstream publications such as the *Guardian*, as a producer of documentaries for the National Geographic Channel, and as author of a dozen provocative books that challenge mainstream scientific beliefs. In the 2000s Temple began promoting what he called the moat theory.

According to Temple the erosion on the sphinx was caused by water but not precipitation that fell from the sky. Instead, he believes the sphinx was once surrounded by water. The body and head of the statue formed an island surrounded by a moat like those placed around medieval castles. The water in the moat was diverted from the Nile River into the three-sided pit where the sphinx was carved. The high wall of the Sphinx Temple in front of the statue formed the fourth side of the artificial lake.

Temple bases his theory on the presence of a drainage channel, about 5 feet (1.5 m) deep and 6 feet (2 m) wide, that stretches between Khafre's pyramid and the sphinx. Most Egyptologists believe the channel, which could divert large quantities of rainwater when heavy downpours occurred, was used to drain water away from the pyramids. Temple believes the channel was used to replenish the water in the Sphinx Moat.

Like other theories, the Sphinx Moat concept has been called into question. Schoch points out that the erosion in the sphinx enclosure is uneven, heavier on one end than the other. This is due to rainfall patterns rather than pooled water, which would create a different type of erosion. Whatever the case, the Sphinx Moat is only one of Temple's controversial theories.

A Jackal-Headed Guardian

Temple also argues that the Sphinx was shaped into a lion's body and human head relatively late in ancient Egyptian history. He points out a well-known fact that no mention of the sphinx is found in ancient manuscripts. Temple states, "I would say that the reason for that is that people have been looking for the wrong things. Texts referring to a lion with a man's head will not be found because that is not what the Sphinx was."[39]

Temple believes the statue was originally created in the shape of a jackal to honor the god Anubis. Jackals are smallish wolves that belong to the canine family. The Greeks considered jackals to be half wolf, half dog. In ancient Egyptian religion, Anubis was the deity of mummification and the afterlife. As long ago as 3100 BC, Anubis was portrayed as a doglike creature crouching on a burial chamber with all four paws pointed forward, keeping watchful attention with open eyes and large, erect ears.

> **Did You Know?**
>
> Construction engineer Robert Bauval believes the Great Sphinx and the pyramids in the Giza region were constructed in patterns that mirror various constellations in the night sky.

The role of Anubis in the mummification and funeral process was extremely important. Ancient Egyptians believed that each person had a vital life force called a *ka* which extended back through previous generations all the way to the gods of creation. The *ka* temporarily left the body upon death, while priests prepared and trans-

One researcher suggests that the original head of the Great Sphinx was built in the shape of a jackal to honor the god Anubis and that it was replaced later by the more familiar human head. A figure wearing an Anubis mask, left, appears in this wall painting from the tomb of Tutankhamun.

formed the corpse into a mummy. Egyptians believed that after the human body was preserved as a mummy, the *ka* would return to it.

Mummification was a long, solemn process that could take as long as 70 days and was originally performed only on pharaohs, royals, and priests. During mummification the brains and other organs were removed, the body was packed in a salt called natron, and embalming fluids were applied to preserve the skin and body interior. The body was wrapped in layers of linen strips with jewel-encrusted magical charms. During the mummification ceremonies, the leading priest wore a mask of Anubis. After the process was finished, the jackal-headed priest performed a ceremony called the Opening of the Mouth. Dressed as Anubis, he ritually opened the mouth, eyes, nostrils, and ears of the mummy so that the *ka* could reenter the body.

While no images of a half-lion, half-human sphinx existed until around 2500 BC, statues, amulets, and pictures of Anubis number in the thousands. Because of the god's role in embalming, cemeteries, and the afterlife, Anubis is painted on coffins and burial chambers. Anubis plays a prominent role in the *Pyramid Texts*, ancient religious scrolls written to guide the pharaoh into the afterlife. In the *Pyramid Texts* Anubis calls the pharaoh forth and grants him sustenance and eternal life.

The pyramids were built as tombs for pharaohs, and as Mark Lehner writes, "when we visit the pyramids we walk on ancient graveyards."[40] This is the basis for Temple's theory. It would make perfect sense to create a giant statue of Anubis to watch over the elaborate cemetery that is Giza. This impression came over Temple when he originally visited the area:

As I looked at the Sphinx that first time, noting the straight back of the creature and the complete absence of leonine features or characteristics of any kind, I was struck by the fact that I appeared to be staring at a dog. . . . There it sits crouching on its belly, and it is a dog. And what is more, Anubis was frequently represented in precisely that posture throughout the thousands of years of Egyptian art. . . . He lies in precisely the manner of the Sphinx.[41]

Temple backs his theory with drawings that superimpose the long muzzle and tall ears of the jackal-headed Anubis over the existing head of the Great Sphinx. These drawings make it appear as if the jackal head is in much better proportion to the body. Also reasonable to believe is that these features, because of their length and weight, could have easily broken off or been purposely removed from the original stone carving.

The Martian Sphinx

Other theories of the origin of the sphinx have been suggested as well. Perhaps the most bizarre theory concerning the sphinx has its roots in the 1970s. In August 1975 the US space agency, NASA, launched a space probe called *Viking 1* on a journey to Mars. While a small vehicle called a lander explored the Martian surface, the *Viking* orbiter circled the red planet for six years. During this time, the spacecraft sent over 52,000 images of Mars back to Earth. In 1977 Richard Hoagland, a science consultant to CBS News, CNN, and NASA, was studying the *Viking* photos when he noticed a massive face that seemed to be carved onto a mountain in the Cydonia region of Mars. The image had a startling resemblance to the Great Sphinx. Hoagland, who also believes that space aliens regularly visit Earth, called the image the Face of Mars. He believes it was part of a city built by an advanced civilization. NASA contends that the Face of Mars is an illusion caused by light and shadows. Hoagland asserts that the government knows the Martian sphinx was created by space aliens, but it is hiding the information to prevent widespread panic on Earth.

The Face on Mars gained greater attention in 1982 when two former NASA computer engineers, Vincent DePietro and Gregory Molenaar, used a computer to digitally enhance the *Viking* photos. In pictures produced by the team, the Martian sphinx appears to be

> ## Did You Know?
> Those who believe the sphinx is carved on a mountain on Mars also claim that several Martian pyramids exist about 7 miles (11.2 km) away. These formations, which scientists say are mountains, are 10 times the height of the Great Pyramid of Giza.

huge—2,000 feet (610 m) high, 1.6 miles (2.5 km) long, and 1.2 miles (2 km) wide.

In the decades after his discovery of the Face of Mars, Hoagland became a proponent of the theory that the Great Sphinx and the pyramids were not built by Egyptians. Rather, he contends, they were built by an advanced race of space aliens that also constructed the Martian sphinx. According to Hoagland:

> [The pyramids and sphinx] are not classic Egyptian . . . they're much, much older, maybe . . . 13 thousand years old or maybe 50 thousand years old, or maybe even older than that, because there's no way to date the stone. It is conceivable that we're dealing with a high tech civilization that placed these [monuments] there for purposes that have nothing to do with the classic Egyptian mythologies and ceremonies. . . . [The] Egyptians that came much, much later [in] the last 6,000 years, merely took advantage of preexisting monuments built by their great, great, great, great, great, great ancestors and created ceremonies to explain the ineffable, the enigmatic, the mysterious.[42]

An Enigma with Many Sides

The designers and builders of the ancient Egyptian sphinx have baffled countless generations long after their society disappeared. In this way the sphinx is an enigma with many sides. It undeniably exists as a rock in the desert, it acts as a symbol of monsters and mystery, and it represents human artistic skills and imagination.

Like blowing grains of sand, a whirlwind of ideas swirls around the Great Sphinx of Giza. Perhaps some of the questions about the monument will be answered in the coming years. Until that time, ancient history will be reexamined, dissected, and rewritten rightly or wrongly. If the sphinx knows cosmic truths, it is not telling. The sphinx conveys thousands of ideas but remains as silent as the desert stars.

Source Notes

Chapter One: The Egyptian Sphinx

1. Quoted in A.H. Sayce, ed., "Records of the Past," Internet Archive, 2010. www.archive.org.
2. Quoted in Evan Hadingham, "Riddle of the Sphinx," *Cosmos*, April 2010. www.cosmosmagazine.com.
3. Kasia Szpakowska, "The Dream Stela of Thutmosis IV," *Nova*, PBS, January 1, 2010. www.pbs.org.
4. Mark Lehner, *The Complete Pyramids*. London: Thames and Hudson, 1997, p. 132.
5. Lehner, *The Complete Pyramids*, p. 132.
6. Quoted in Hadingham, "Riddle of the Sphinx."
7. Hadingham, "Riddle of the Sphinx."
8. Quoted in Ciar Byrne, "Answer Found to Riddle of Sphinx," *Independent* (London), December 11, 2004. www.independent.co.uk.
9. Metropolitan Museum of Art, "Sphinx of Hatshepsut," April 5, 2011. www.metmuseum.org.
10. Quoted in Desmond Stewart, *The Pyramids and Sphinx*. New York: Newsweek, 1971, pp. 61–62.

Chapter Two: The Sphinx in Classical Greece

11. Herodotus, *History*. Chicago: University of Chicago Press, 1987, p. 185.
12. Herodotus, *The Histories of Herodotus*, George Rawlinson, ed. London: John Murry, 1858, p. 265.
13. Quoted in J. Michael Padgett, ed., *The Centaur's Smile: The Human Animal in Early Greek Art*. New Haven, CT: Yale University Press, 2004, p. 49.
14. Homer, *The Odyssey*, Internet Classics Archive, 2009. http://classics.mit.edu.
15. Hugh G. Evelyn-White, trans., *Hesiod, the Homeric Hymns, and Homerica*. Cambridge, MA: Harvard University Press, 1995, p. 47.

16. Willis Goth Regier, *Book of the Sphinx*. Lincoln: University of Nebraska Press, 2004, pp. 41–42.

17. Quoted in Padgett, *The Centaur's Smile*, p. 79.

18. Regier, *Book of the Sphinx*, p. 42.

19. Delphi Archaeological Museum, Delphi, Naxian Sphinx (sculpture), Perseus Digital Library, April 14, 2011. www.perseus.tufts.edu.

20. Quoted in Padgett, *The Centaur's Smile*, p. 282.

21. Quoted in Jenifer Neils, *The Parthenon: From Antiquity to the Present*. New York: Cambridge University Press, 2005, p. 263.

22. Quoted in Padgett, *The Centaur's Smile*, p. 82.

Chapter Three: Sphinxes in the Modern Era

23. Quoted in Robert Temple and Olivia Temple, *The Sphinx Mystery*. Rochester, VT: Inner Traditions, 2009, p. 457.

24. Quoted in Temple and Temple, *The Sphinx Mystery*, p. 453.

25. Lord Balcarres, *Donatello*. New York: Charles Scribner's Sons, 1903, p. 63.

26. Robert Penn Warren, *The Grotesque in Art and Literature: Theological Reflections*. Grand Rapids, MI: Wm. B. Eerdmans, 1997, pp. 6–7.

27. Nicolas Grimal, *A History of Ancient Egypt*. Cambridge, MA: Blackwell, 1992, p. 6.

28. English Russia, "Sphinx St. Petersburg," September 7, 2007. http://englishrussia.com.

29. Quoted in Regier, *Book of the Sphinx*, p. 182.

30. Christiane Zivie-Coche, *Sphinx: History of a Monument*. Ithaca, NY: Cornell University Press, 2002, p. 16.

31. Regier, *Book of the Sphinx*, p. 98.

32. Percy Bysshe Shelley, *Prometheus Unbound*. Cambridge, MA: Harvard College Library, 1903, pp. 19–20.

33. Regier, *Book of the Sphinx*, p. 154.

Chapter Four: Ancient Monument, Modern Theories

34. Robert M. Schoch, "The Great Sphinx," Official Website of Robert M. Schoch, 2011. www.robertschoch.com.

35. Schoch, "The Great Sphinx."

36. Quoted in Graham Hancock and Robert Bauval, *The Message of the Sphinx*. New York: Random House, 1996, pp. 15–16. www.robertschoch.net.

37. Robert M. Schoch, "Redating the Great Sphinx of Giza," *Circular Times*, 2009.

38. Quoted in Graham Hancock, "Tunnels and Chambers Under the Great Sphinx," The Modern Riddle of the Sphinx, Biblioteca Pleyades. www.bibliotecapleyades.net.

39. Temple and Temple, *The Sphinx Mystery*, p. 202.

40. Lehner, *The Complete Pyramids*, p. 22.

41. Temple and Temple, *The Sphinx Mystery*, p. 204.

42. Richard Hoagland, "On Secrets and Cover-Ups in Egypt," Biblioteca Pleyades, 2006. www.bibliotecapleyades.net.

For Further Exploration

Books

Megan E. Bryant, *Oh My Gods! A Look-It-Up Guide to the Gods of Mythology*. New York: Franklin Watts, 2010.

Pete DiPrimio, *The Sphinx*. Hockessin, DE: Mitchell Lane, 2011.

Stuart A. Kallen, *Ancient Egypt*. San Diego: ReferencePoint Press, 2012.

Sophia Kelly, *What a Beast! A Look-It-Up Guide to the Monsters and Mutants of Mythology*. New York: Franklin Watts, 2010.

Bimba Landmann, *The Incredible Voyage of Ulysses*. Los Angeles: J. Paul Getty Museum, 2010.

Willis Goth Regier, *Book of the Sphinx*. Lincoln: University of Nebraska Press, 2004.

Websites

Ancient Egypt History (www.ancient-egypt-history.com). This site contains articles and information about ancient Egypt encompassing the pyramids and Great Sphinx, pharaohs and queens, temples, and monuments.

Ancient Greece (www.ancientgreece.com). A comprehensive exploration of the art, architecture, history, wars, geography, and mythology of ancient Greece.

DrHawass.com (www.drhawass.com). The website of internationally renowned Egyptologist Zahi Hawass, who served as Egypt's secretary general of the Supreme Council of Antiquities and directed ongoing excavations at Giza, Saqqara, and in the Valley of the Kings. In addition to highlighting a wide range of Egyptian antiquities, Hawass also supplied continuous updates about work at the Avenue of the Sphinxes in Luxor.

Egypt: Land of Eternity (http://ib205.tripod.com/book.html). An extremely detailed site published by British Egyptologist Ian Bolton, featuring assorted information about ancient Egyptian kings and queens, gods and goddesses, mythology, tombs, and monuments.

Redating the Sphinx (www.davidpbillington.net/sphinx2.html). This site published key articles related to the ongoing debate over the Predynastic Sphinx concept with photos, maps, and links to sites run by key proponents of the theory as well as skeptics and detractors.

Index

Note: Pages in boldface indicate illustrations.

Picture Credits

Cover: Thinkstock/AbleStock.com

Athena Parthenos, Statue from Parthenon, Athens (color engraving), French School, (19th century)/Bibliotheque des Arts Decoratifs, Paris, France/Archives Charmet/The Bridgeman Art Library International: 35

Bettmann/Corbis: 42

© Elio Ciol/Corbis: 39

DeA Picture Library/Art Resource, NY: 53

© National Geographic Society/Corbis: 17

Oedipus and the Sphinx, 1808 (oil on canvas), Ingres, Jean Auguste Dominique (1780-1867)/Louvre, Paris, France/The Bridgman Art Library International: 46

The Questioner of the Sphinx (oil on canvas), Vedder, Elihu (1836–1923)/Worcester Art Museum, Massachusetts, USA/The Bridgman Art Library International: 49

Réunion des Musées Nationaux/Art Resource, NY: 27

© Fulvio Roiter/Corbis: 10

Thinkstock/Hemera: 7, 15, 22, 57

Thinkstock/iStockphoto: 25

© Sandro Vannini/Corbis: 63

About the Author

Stuart A. Kallen is the author of more than 250 nonfiction books for children and young adults. He has written on topics ranging from the theory of relativity to the history of rock and roll. In addition, Kallen has written award-winning children's videos and television scripts. In his spare time, he is a singer/songwriter/guitarist in San Diego.